DATE DUE

THE LEWIS AND CLARK EXPEDITION

THE
LEWIS AND CLARK
EXPEDITION

★

by RICHARD L. NEUBERGER

Illustrated by WINOLD REISS

THIS SPECIAL EDITION IS PRINTED AND DISTRIBUTED
BY ARRANGEMENT WITH THE ORIGINATORS AND
PUBLISHERS OF LANDMARK BOOKS
RANDOM HOUSE, INC. NEW YORK
BY
E. M. HALE AND COMPANY
EAU CLAIRE, WISCONSIN

For

ANN AND KATIE GOODSELL

Two little girls who
live on the trail of
Lewis and Clark.

CONTENTS

THE LEWIS AND CLARK EXPEDITION

1

Last Letters Home

IN THE FLICKERING LIGHT OF HIS CAMPFIRE, a soldier of the United States Army was writing a letter. He did not wear the brass buttons and dashing uniform which we usually associate with a soldier. His clothes were of soiled buckskin. Ragged fringes of buckskin ran down his sleeves and legs. They swayed as the soldier moved. On his feet were moccasins of Indian pattern. Nearby, a long rifle leaned against a tree. Tied to the gunstock by a thong was a powder horn. Over the muzzle of the rifle, the soldier had tossed his coonskin cap.

Sergeant John Ordway, tall and lean, slowly pushed his goose-quill pen across the sheet of paper.

"Honored parents," the letter began, "I now take this opportunity to let you know where I am and what I am doing. I am on an expedition to the westward with Captain Lewis and Captain Clark, who are appointed by the President of the United States to go through the interior parts of North America. We shall ascend the Missouri River and then go by land to the Western Ocean. I do not know when I can write to you again."

The letter was to be posted to distant Bow, New Hampshire, where the parents of 28-year-old John Ordway lived. The sergeant's thoughts were serious as he sealed the envelope. Had he seen his father and mother for the last time?

His home in New Hampshire was far from this encampment that had been built just out of sight of the frontier settlement of St. Louis. The grove of alder trees where Ordway sat writing was pin-pointed with many campfires. Beside these dancing cones of flame, other young men in deerskin were putting pen to paper. There might never be another chance to write to loved ones back home.

This was the foggy night of May 13, 1804. On the next day the first party to attempt the crossing of the western part of our country would start on its journey.

Draymen were unloading heavy crates from wagons and stacking them beneath the trees. An Army quartermaster checked off each bundle.

"Pewter looking-glasses, fifteen dozen," he would call.

And the draymen with the crate would repeat, "Pewter looking-glasses, fifteen dozen."

This went on far into the night. When the Army man called, "Fancy bracelets, 500," a drayman murmured to his companion:

"Them's for the Indians. Plenty of wild ones up-river, I hear. Some of the tribes have never seen a white man. Maybe these trinkets will keep 'em in their place. Glad I ain't betting my life on it, though."

An air of excitement gripped the sprawling encampment, for the soldiers of the backwoods were awaiting the arrival of the man who would be their leader—Meriwether Lewis. No ordinary Army captain had been put in charge of the project. Although only thirty years old, Meriwether Lewis was the private secretary to President Thomas Jefferson. Indeed, Lewis was now on his way by horseback directly from the White House in Washington, D. C.

"And he's commissioned in my outfit, too," boasted John Ordway. "First Infantry regiment—best outfit in the Army!"

In his kitbag Captain Lewis was said to carry secret orders from the President. These orders would not be opened until the party was deep in the wilderness. Only a few days earlier the flag of France had drifted down the pole in the public square at New Orleans, to be replaced by the Stars and Stripes. This was the result of the Louisiana

Purchase, arranged by Mr. Jefferson's ambassador in Paris. The United States had paid France $15,000,000 for one million square miles of land west of the Mississippi River. This was five times the area of France itself.

Yet there were some men in Congress who whispered that the hopes of the President went far beyond the boundaries of Louisiana Territory. Could this be what the secret orders were about?

The soldiers of the expedition lay in their blankets, but sleep would not come. Who could sleep on the eve of this greatest of all adventures?

Sergeant John Ordway wondered if ever again he would dance the quadrille with slim and pretty Deborah Tillson in the New Hampshire township where they had gone to school. Would 17-year-old George Shannon, sipping tea from a tin mug, get back to his fields of tobacco and barley in Ohio? What experiences must they all go through before the nine young pioneers from Kentucky would hunt once more in their native hills? They had been signed up by Captain Clark because of their craft in the forests.

Would the party meet prehistoric monsters, wild and shaggy elephants and dragons breathing fire? Were there really jagged peaks of rock-salt which glittered like glass and blinded the eye? And what lay past the source of the mighty Missouri, where white men had never been? Did the earth drop off into boundless space?

These things make us smile today. Yet in 1804 Americans knew far less about the land west of St. Louis than we do now about the Congo jungle or the Amazon Valley, or even the ice fields of the Antarctic. In John

Ordway's knapsack was a map that had been printed in a newspaper called the *New York Gazette*. On this map, everything west of his campfire near St. Louis was as white as one of his mother's fine linen tablecloths at home. There was not a river or lake or mountain range. It was just blank space. Several Senators accused President Jefferson of sending the thirty-three men of the party to certain death in a search for "the unknown and the unknowable."

However, the anger of the President's political enemies was greater than their concern for the men of the expedition. As a result, Congress allowed the expedition only $2,500 for expenses. This meant that no doctor could be taken along, although the party might be gone for years. Only fifty-five dollars could be spent on medicines. The men were to get their wages from the War Department because they all had Army rank. Private soldiers would get five dollars a month. Sergeants like John Ordway would be paid eight dollars. Lewis and Clark each would receive eighty dollars a month.

This, too, puzzles us today and we shake our heads in amazement. A private in the Army now earns more money than Captain Meriwether Lewis, private secretary to the President, was paid in 1804. But we must remember that the United States was a very young nation when its eager explorers made ready to break camp and depart from St. Louis long ago.

California was then barely a name. Thomas Jefferson had heard of "the Great River Oregon," which seafaring men said was bigger than the Missouri. This "great river" was also called the Columbia, but its direction was a mystery. Surely, somewhere, it joined the Western Ocean, the blue Pacific.

And Indians muttered at the council fire about the Shining or Rocky Mountains that scraped the sky. These mountains were believed to be three times the height of the White Mountains or the Appalachians. John Ordway thought of the timbered summits which looked down on his home in New Hampshire. Three times that high! He grinned a satisfied smile, as he finally napped just before dawn.

Such mountains could never be!

2

The Start of a Great Adventure

LET US WATCH THESE FIRST OF ALL WESTBOUND white men, as they sail up the broad Missouri River.

In the lead were two narrow open row-boats that tested the sandbars and shallows, and shoved off floating logs. Behind these small craft came a 55-foot keel boat. Private George Drouillard, whose parents had been French, called it a *bateau*.

This boat was moved upstream by a flapping canvas sail and twenty-two heavy oars. Eleven oars were on each side. To children peering wide-eyed from the riverbank in St. Louis, the keel boat looked like Viking vessels they had seen pictured in their schoolbooks.

"Hurrah! Hurrah!" they shouted from shore, for they realized a great event was taking place.

The keel boat had two crowded cabins, and it was surrounded by wooden breastworks four feet high. Behind these breastworks, men could fire their long rifles and still be safe from spears and arrows. No one knew what the supposedly fierce Indians of the plains would do when they saw for the first time the banner which flew from the stately mast of the keel boat. This banner of red, white and blue was the American flag with its seventeen stars, for already Vermont, Kentucky, Tennessee and Ohio had been added to the original thirteen colonies.

Never were boats piled so high with goods. Each time a soldier stirred in his seat, he had to move a bundle or crate. Today airplanes deliver supplies to explorers. Provisions can come from anywhere on earth in a few hours. But these men voyaging up the Missouri River had only the supplies they could take with them.

Few other parties ever have been so completely on their own. All their rations had cost only $224. These included soup stock, flour, tea, cornmeal and salt and pepper. The rest of their food would have to result from the steady aim of the hunters and the sure skill of the fishermen. Just one soldier in our time often has supplies worth more than this!

When the young explorers were past the neighboring village of St. Charles, they found themselves in a strange new world. Only a handful of traders had been beyond St. Charles, and soon even the comfortable camps of the traders were left behind.

Sergeant Ordway would not forget the smiling woman, with a little girl at her apron strings, who gave him a cold glass of milk in St. Charles. He remembered that the little girl's name was "Sarah" and that she had long, braided pigtails which ended in bright blue ribbons. The sergeant would drink no milk again for two years, but he would think of little pigtailed Sarah when he wished for another cool white glass from that generous kitchen.

And some day, when she was wrinkled and gray, Sarah would tell grandchildren of her own how she had watched the frontiersmen in buckskin going through St. Charles on that first journey to Oregon.

"Goodbye! Goodbye!" she had shouted until the three boats vanished from sight around a bend in the river.

The men of Lewis and Clark were entering the homeland of hundreds of savage Indian tribes. Their lives would depend upon the friendliness of the Indians. Could thirty-three men—even men armed with rifles—stand against thousands of red-skinned warriors?

So the cabins of the keel boat bulged with presents. Imagine bales bursting with beads, brooches, glittering rings, striped shirts of calico, tinkling bells, cans of colored paint and sturdy brass kettles. There were 4,600 needles and seventy yards of beautiful red cloth to delight an Indian maiden's fanciest taste.

Gleaming medals bore the carved likeness of Thomas Jefferson. These were for the chiefs. Lewis and Clark were ordered to enter into treaties between the Great White Father and his new subjects. Trade goods would smooth the way. After all, these Indians had never before heard of the United States of America.

And what if there really were the Shining Mountains, many times as high as any which Americans yet had seen in their native land? No boats could ascend such peaks. Their fleet would have to be left behind. Only wiry and nimble Indian ponies could get their heavy supplies over those summits.

18

"The ponies must not be stolen. They must be bought, fairly and honestly," Lewis told the men. His stern expression showed that he meant every word of this command.

But more than their own lives depended upon successful passage through the hunting grounds of the Indians. The life of their country was also at stake. A race for empire was on. To the north the British explorers, Alexander Mackenzie and Simon Fraser, were searching for the capes and beaches where "the great River Oregon" flowed into the sea. Spaniards were poking up the coast from the land dimly known as California.

Possession of Louisiana Territory might never take place unless the American flag was first to wave at the mouth of "the Great River Oregon." And Mr. Jefferson did not think the United States could survive if it was pinched into a narrow strip along the

Atlantic Ocean. Its rivals would be too strong for a small nation to hold back.

So row, row hard for America, you soldiers in the boats with Lewis and Clark!

Woodsmen from Virginia bent their backs beside carpenters from Pennsylvania and farmers from Connecticut. John Potts, fat and jolly, was Dutch. Cruzat and Drouillard were French. The ancestors of Hugh McNeal had sailed from Scotland in quest of opportunity. Patrick Gass and William Bratton, alert in tight places, were Irish.

The expedition was a true cross-section of the free country just then coming into being. Rich and poor alike swung the oars. John Shields was a Kentucky blacksmith, but a wealthy Ohio farm family had reared George Shannon.

Potts was forty-one and Gass was gray-headed at thirty-three. But eight of the explorers could not vote, for they had yet to reach the age of twenty-one. Youngest of all was 16-year-old John Colter from Pittsburgh, who one day on a lonely trap-line would discover the wonders of the Yellowstone. And near William Clark in the first boat crouched his brawny Negro servant, York, whose strength equalled that of any other two men in the party.

Study now the two leaders of this fateful expedition. Never were faithful friends such opposites.

Meriwether Lewis, the senior captain, was a silent and brooding man. He said very little. Yet when he spoke, others listened attentively. Determination was his main trait. He never let his eye stray from the goal. Thin and lithe, he slipped through the woods with the grace of an Indian. The fact that he was a distant relative of General

21

George Washington added to the awe in which others of the party held him.

But silence never characterized William Clark! He chattered constantly on the trail. "Get along now, Frazier. Puffing, Thompson? Too many boss ribs of buffalo at supper, I'll wager! You'll be as fat as our friend Potts come Sunday! Short rations for you all the rest of the week."

A head of bright red hair cast a constant glow on Clark's merry face. Like Lewis, he kept a diary of all the happenings from sunrise until he sought his blankets at night. Clark could not spell, and frequently he had to get help with words from the better-educated Ordway, who had been assigned by Lewis to keep the accounts of the expedition.

But Ordway was not always handy, and so Captain Clark wrote "brease" for breeze, "jentle" instead of gentle and "butifull" when he meant beautiful.

Clark was thirty-four when the expedition started. This made him four years older than Lewis, although most people took their ages to be the exact opposite of this. The lively Clark actually seemed much younger than his solemn companion.

In the choking heat of the prairie summer, sweat rolled off the men's backs as they tugged at the clumsy oars. Buckskin jackets were flung into the bottom of the boats. Shoulders and arms were burned as brown as the feathers of a grouse. Peter Cruzat, stacking crates in one of the cabins, picked up his battered violin. Even the somber Lewis ventured a thin smile when the words of a rollicking French *voyageur* song of the moment came across the Missouri's waves:

23

"At the clear running fountain.
   Sauntering by one day,

"I found it so compelling,
   I bathed without delay.

"Under an oak tree's foliage,
   I dried the damp away,

"Dried the damp away. . . ."

3

Death on the Missouri

Bear!

In the lengthening shadows of the afternoon, with the boats tied up along the riverbank, Clark and Drouillard were hunting. Suddenly they saw a bear's familiar hump in a swaying thicket of honeysuckle.

Bear steaks and rump stews were welcome in the camp kettles, and the fur would keep someone warm in the bleak winter ahead.

Clark fired his gun first, but this bear did not drop. It reared with a roar out of the underbrush and rushed at its tormenters. Drouillard fired, yet still the bear did not fall. Clark was looking down the red mouth, full of dripping fangs, when he pumped a third ball into the beast.

This was more than the explorers had bargained for. The roly-poly bears of New England rarely required even a second shot. Clark took refuge behind a tree, and Drouillard discharged still a fourth pellet into the snarling target. Clark had been given a few precious seconds in which to reload, and for a fifth time the animal was hit.

But now their shot and powder had been scattered across the ground in the melee. The two frightened men dropped their guns and leaped from a high bank into the Missouri. They swam to a sand bar and crawled out, limp and dripping. Drouillard peered nervously over his shoulder.

"Captain, look!"

And no wonder at his excitement! The bear, with five piercing balls in its carcass, was swimming after them! Clark and Drouillard drew their hunting knives and huddled on the far edge of the sand bar. They would battle to the end against such a bear as white men probably had never seen before.

The bear plodded out of the water and onto the beach, its head weaving from side to side like a pendulum. Then, slowly, it toppled over. Shaken and trembling, the two frontiersmen at last examined their kill.

"It'd make three of the bears I used to hunt in Ohio," said the astonished Clark.

The bear's fur was a grizzled reddish-brown. Its claws were like pitchforks. The bear weighed between 500 and 600 pounds and measured 8 feet 7½ inches from nose to hind feet. This pelt would keep more than one man warm!

Americans had discovered the grizzly bear. *Ursus horribilis*—"the frightful bear," Captain Lewis called the discovery. And now the men murmured around the bubbling tea-pot about shaggy elephants and flaming dragons. What couldn't turn up in this vast and endless realm, where there were bears the size of a coach-and-four?

We take for granted today the wild creatures which roam our continent. But to Lewis and Clark they were as strange as some of the weird fish from the very bottom of the ocean are to us now. Antelope, prairie dogs, mountain goats, bighorn sheep, grizzlies, silver fox, marten, white cranes and many species of duck and geese—all these were unknown until Lewis and Clark went west.

The captains scribbled constantly in their notebooks. What a tale they would have to tell when they returned! They made crude sketches of a fleeing antelope and a snarling grizzly bear. Ordway added drawings to his account papers. We must remember that these men had no cameras, not even an old-fashioned kodak with bellows and cloth hood.

Clark cut out the heart of the great grizzly lying dead on the sand bar. "As big as the heart of a fullgrown ox," he said, and called on the others to witness this astounding fact.

They signed their names at the bottom of the page in his diary where he told how the bear had swum the river after being hit five times by rifle balls. That page and the pelt of the grizzly would be their only proof if ever they stood in the presence of Mr. Jefferson at the White House and related the afternoon's amazing happenings.

But even St. Louis seemed far off to Private John Newman, who stared in fright back down the twisting Missouri. What awaited them in this lonely land? Newman disobeyed an order to stand guard at night, and instantly a court-martial was called in the wilderness. Only privates sat in judgment on their fellow soldier.

"Have you reached a verdict?" asked Clark.

"Seventy-five lashes," answered Private Werner.

While a wandering tribe of peaceful Arikara Indians watched in horror, Newman more than twice ran between two long lines of waiting soldiers. They flailed at his bare and bleeding back with willow switches as he passed.

With Drouillard interpreting, the chief of the Arikaras asked the reason for this grim punishment.

"We are sent by the Great White Father to make friends with you," Lewis replied. "We are strangers in a far land. If we do not stand by each other, all our lives will be in danger. Even our country may be in peril. He who defies a command must pay the price, for he has endangered his comrades. But this judgment is rendered only by his equals."

The old chief listened gravely as Drouillard explained what Lewis had said.

As Ordway looked at Newman, slumped on the seat of one of the rowboats, he wondered if it was true that bad luck came in pairs. He did not have long to wait.

Charles Floyd, one of the three Army sergeants on the expedition, complained of a gnawing pain in his stomach. He lay in the cabin of the keel boat and writhed in agony.

At the order of President Jefferson, Lewis had visited the great Philadelphia surgeon, Benjamin Rush, before the westward journey began. Dr. Rush, a signer of the Declaration of Independence, had instructed him carefully in first-aid and in ministering to the sick. He also had given Lewis a great quantity of pills and powders.

"Alas! If only Dr. Rush were here to instruct me now," bewailed Lewis as he bent over the stricken Floyd.

The condition of the sergeant became worse at dawn, after a night of suffering. His pain increased. Tonics and potions only added to his misery. He clutched at the captain's hand to keep from screaming. Then his strength seemed to fade. "I am going away," he whispered hoarsely.

Lewis felt the cold pulse and his lean face became masklike. "We will bury the sergeant on the high bluff across the river," he said.

Sioux City, Iowa, now hums and thrives near the grave of this first of all American soldiers to die in the western half of the continent. But on the day that Charles Floyd was buried, his thirty-two comrades stood silent and alone in an alien land. Even Lewis' big Newfoundland dog, Scannon, sorrowfully eyed the cross of cedar before they all filed off the rocky bluff.

Lewis wrote in his diary that Floyd had died of "the colic." But we think now that it probably was appendicitis, with a burst appendix pouring infection into the sergeant's body.

The episode serves to show us how poorly the expedition was prepared for the perils of a hostile region. It had no doctor, few drugs, no surgical supplies, and no way of ever sending for these things in an emergency.

Lewis had divided the party into three separate squads, so some order could continue even if they were disorganized by an attack. This meant a third sergeant was needed to replace Floyd. The captain called Sergeants John Ordway and Nat Pryor from the circle at the campfire.

"I have the power under Army regulations to appoint the new sergeant," he said. "Yet I think it would be better for the spirit of the men after this tragedy to have it done by free election."

With neither Lewis nor Clark taking part, the soldiers nominated Privates Gass, Gibson and Bratton. Ringing speeches were made in the night. The men pretended they were at conventions of the Federalist or Democratic political parties. Ordway and Pryor distributed pieces of blank paper and passed around a quill pen. When the tallying was finished, Patrick Gass had been elevated to the rank of sergeant in the United States Army and his pay increased from five to eight dollars a month.

For the first time Americans had voted in the vast domain they would one day rule by the ballot.

4

The Shining Mountains

"ALMIGHTY GOD, WE THANK THEE FOR HAVING brought us thus far on our perilous journey. . . ."

It was Christmas Day, 1804, and the expedition lay snug and cozy inside Fort Mandan. The log stockade had been built with ax and saw as winter swept like a scythe across the northern plains. One day these plains would be the state of North Dakota, but the frontiersmen saw them as fluffy white pillows of snow, unbroken by track or trail.

William Clark led the explorers in grateful prayer, for they had come 1,600 winding miles by water from St. Louis. There was a feast of smoked turkey and corn pudding, with the rare treat of a glass of brandy apiece for a hearty toast.

"To Mr. Thomas Jefferson, the President of the United States!" cried Lewis, leading the tribute.

Down the long wooden tables echoed the toast: "To Mr. Thomas Jefferson!"

Home-made Christmas presents were exchanged—a bundle of eagle feathers for Ordway, a sprig of red vine maple for Pryor, a string of dried currants for young Colter, a pair of ragged gloves of buffalo hide for York, plugs of carefully saved tobacco for the captains.

And Lewis spoke everyone's silent thoughts when he asked, "Where shall we celebrate another Christmas? Will we give thanks on the sandy shores of the great Western Ocean?"

This festive day of the curious white men was watched in wonder by a black-haired Indian girl with two long braids down her straight back. Her dark eyes were bright and expressive, and she had teeth that gleamed like jewels. She was called Sacajawea, "the Bird Woman." At nineteen she was the wife of Toussaint Charbonneau, son of a Sioux mother and a French-Canadian father.

Charbonneau had trudged into the fort and offered his services as an interpreter for twenty-five dollars a month. He also wanted ammunition for his gun, which was useless without powder and ball. These were the first people he had met in the wilderness who could restore his hunting equipment.

In the land of the fierce Sioux, Lewis was worried over his relationships with the Indians. Drouillard had difficulty following the sing-song language of the prairie tribes. Often pow-wows broke up because Lewis and the chiefs could not understand each other. He had been forced to give away his own gold-braided captain's uniform, because an important brave took offense at Drouillard's clumsy translation of the Indian tongue.

The uniform was dear to Lewis and he felt heartsick when he parted with it. But he was under orders from the President to avoid trouble with the Indians at all costs. This particular Indian leader demanded the uniform when Drouillard interpreted his words incorrectly.

Only by disconnected rumors had Lewis learned later that the Sioux hoped to wipe out the strange invaders. This was why Fort Mandan was built stout and sturdy, with many loopholes for rifles. The iron swivel gun from the prow of the keel boat had been mounted menacingly at the gate of the fort.

Lewis needed an interpreter, yet he told Charbonneau, "We're heading into wild country where no white man ever has dreamed of going before. We can't be slowed down by a woman."

"My wife is brave and strong," answered Charbonneau. "She is better on the trail than a man. She can carry a full load. And she is a Shoshone. Her home is to the west— many leagues west. She was stolen from her tribe as a young girl by the Minnetarees and sold as a slave."

Lewis still hesitated, yet he was wavering. The Shoshones were the legendary tribe which dwelt in the very heart of the Shining Mountains. Perhaps this copper-skinned Indian girl might help the expedition get ponies.

Soon still another member was added to the party. Sacajawea gave birth to a son. The proud father, eager to emphasize his French blood, named the infant "Baptiste." But the merry Clark had no patience with such a fancy name.

"It's too hard to spell in my diary," explained the easy-going captain, and he began referring to the baby as "Pompey." This stemmed from an Indian word *pomp*, meaning "first-born," which indeed Pompey was.

41

And to Sacajawea the captain with red hair said:

"From now on you are going to be 'Janey' in my book. That's a name I can spell, too. Furthermore, you remind me of a very dark and pretty Janey I once knew back in Kentucky."

Sacajawea was far from sure what all this meant, but she was flattered to receive attention from one of the great captains who commanded the marvelous white men. With her papoose on her back, she sat for hours in a log hut at Fort Mandan. Her eyes never strayed as she watched Lewis and Clark stuffing animal heads, pressing leaves and ferns, gluing fish bones to sheets of paper and coating bird feathers with varnish.

"Won't this collection make Mr. Jefferson sit up and take notice?" said Lewis, half to himself.

Sacajawea did not know who Mr. Jefferson was, but she was sure from the tone in the captain's voice that he must be someone extremely important. And she felt important in her own right when Lewis took a string of snake rattles from one of the boxes which was to go to the White House, and gave it to little Pompey for a toy.

At last winter loosened its icy grip on the Missouri and they started out again. Behind them they left not only the safe shelter of Fort Mandan but also the ungainly keel boat. The river was veering off to the westward, and it was becoming too swift and shallow for a large craft. The Missouri clawed at its banks with white-capped talons. And the banks were stiffening into cliffs.

Joe Fields, one of the Kentucky mountaineers, was bitten on the leg by a five-foot rattlesnake, but a blood-letting and some of

Dr. Rush's crystals saved his life. A buffalo stampede crushed several crates of their valuable equipment, and now grizzly bears were everywhere. Lewis issued orders against any man leaving camp alone. It nearly always took two rifles to slay these ferocious animals. Their growls could be heard all through the night.

Clark went hunting with Sacajawea and her husband. A flashflood trapped them in a narrow gully. Charbonneau lost his courage and thought only of escaping with his own skin, but the others clung to a granite ledge and saved the helpless baby, Pompey. In the churning flood, their knapsacks vanished. Clark's knapsack had contained the only compass on the expedition. He and the Indian girl dived for the articles in the cold water, but without success.

This was a stunning blow, yet another soon followed.

The famous government arsenal at Harpers Ferry, Virginia, had forged Lewis a long iron canoe. This had been packed in two pieces on the deck of the keel boat, to be used in the surging upper river. The canoe was named *Experiment* and covered with elk skins to make it float better. But alas for *Experiment!* It could not ride the rough rapids and the elk skins peeled off.

Now they were desperately short of storage space. *Experiment* had been their only small boat with room to stow many supplies. While the men grumbled, Lewis ordered all kinds of equipment to be abandoned. This included practically every souvenir and keepsake.

"But, Captain, that antelope cape was for my best girl in New York City. She lives on Amsterdam Avenue."

"I hope it's nice and warm on Amsterdam Avenue, Thompson," replied Lewis, "because your best girl will never see that antelope cape unless she walks way out here and gets it for herself."

And then the captain added in grave and serious tone: "On our ammunition and our trade goods, all our lives depend. We have none too much of either one, as matters now stand. We will abandon everything else before we leave behind a grain of powder or a single bolt of calico. Is that clearly understood?"

On May 26, 1805, the men no longer thought of their abandoned treasures. Late in the afternoon Lewis climbed a steep hillside while the rowboats continued up the Missouri. Then down to the river came his distant call:

"Halloo!"

He was beckoning to them to ascend the slope. Soon a long file of men in frayed buckskin stood on the crest beside him. The captain gestured with his forefinger toward the west. On the horizon, faint and far off, stretched a jagged line of peaks. They towered far into the sky. Now and then they caught the rays of the setting sun, so the explorers understood at last why the Indians called them "the Shining Mountains."

The white men watched in silence. All that they heard in that moment was the shrill cry of a kingfisher and the murmur of the hurrying Missouri. Never before had Americans seen such high mountains on the soil of North America.

At night, in the glow of the tossing campfire, Lewis wrote slowly and solemnly in his diary:

"I beheld the Rocky Mountains today for

48

the first time. I reflected upon the difficulties which this snowy barrier probably would throw in my way to the ocean. I thought of the sufferings and hardships of myself and party in them. This in some measure counter-balanced the joy I had felt."

Meriwether Lewis closed the notebook and sat staring into the fire until dawn tinted the heavens overhead.

5

Tracking the Missouri
to Its Lair

As the streamliner speeds west today, all
the grand sights of the wide open spaces
have names which thrill and interest us. Behind each name is a story, and very often
it is a story of the America of long ago.

The train rumbles over a steel bridge, and we peer into the railroad folder to learn the name of the river we have crossed. The brightly painted chain of cars twists like a serpent up a narrow pass, and the conductor knows the name of this gorge the train is following.

From the snowy-white tables in the dining car, with their silver sugar bowls and cream pitchers, we look through wide windows. A lordly mountain peak seems to scrape the clouds. The smiling waiter, who makes this run on the train each week, tells us the name of the mountain.

But in the time of Lewis and Clark, none of the landmarks of the American West had been named. All the rivers except the Missouri were just rushing torrents of water. The Rocky Mountains were mere bumps of ice and stone three miles high. The lakes were

51

only lakes, and that was all. The valleys were unknown. Nothing had a name.

Much of the naming was just doing what comes naturally. Lewis and Clark camped on a wooded island where they had to fire guns half the night at hungry grizzly bears with glistening silver-tipped fur. So it became "White Bear Island." The grizzlies have long since been killed or taken to a zoo, but the name of the island has never changed.

Lewis and Clark spied nimble sheep leaping from crag to crag far above the Missouri. The sheep had huge curving horns that nearly formed a circle. No trapeze artist in a circus was ever more graceful than these creatures. The name "Bighorn Sheep" seemed almost to spell itself as Lewis filled another page in his diary.

A broad river poured out of the North and joined the Missouri system. Glacial sources

gave it a cloudy color. "Looks like something I haven't had to drink since we were in St. Charles more than a year ago," said Ordway. "It looks like milk."

"Milk River it shall be!" exclaimed Lewis, and he wrote rapidly in the thick notebook which was always in his kitbag.

It was great fun. Imagine traveling through a land where you could name the mountains and rivers and even the animals, just as it struck your fancy!

In a very few places Indian tribes had given a definite name to some favorite lake or tepee grounds. When Charbonneau told them about this, Lewis and Clark let the Indian names stand. This policy has come down to us through the years. It is why so many states and cities now have names of Indian origin.

But thousands of places still were left for

Lewis and Clark to name. The captains ran through the names of all the members of the expedition, and not even the dead Sergeant Floyd was left out. A river was named for him.

The black-skinned York, mighty of muscle, saw his name given to a deep canyon. The infant son strapped to Sacajawea's strong back actually was honored twice. Clark sighted a lofty column of lava rock and called it "Pompey's Tower," after his own nickname for the baby. But the solemn Lewis always used the real name of the little papoose, so he picked out a "Baptiste Creek" a few miles farther on.

A vast tributary of the Missouri was found to be hemmed in by cliffs streaked with canary color. Here the national pride of the men with French parents came into evidence. They wanted the river to be known as the *Roche*

Jaune. Now we call this foaming stream by its English translation, the Yellowstone.

Never did men have such a chance to please and delight their sweethearts. What girl wouldn't rather have a great river named for her than get roses or chocolate candy?

Rivers and mountains were named for blondes and brunettes far away. Meriwether Lewis thought fondly of his dimpled cousin, Maria Wood, in distant Albemarle, Virginia. Although this southern beauty would not learn of it for several years to come, a magnificent stream in the Rocky Mountains was named "Maria's River" at that instant.

"Martha's River" was the name Clark gave with blushing cheeks to a woodland stream ribbed with roaring rapids. "It's for a certain M. F.," he said. No amount of begging or teasing could get him to tell whose initials these were.

"Like a thousand cannon all firing at once," shouted Ordway, who had served with Federal troops in the Whiskey Rebellion.

Lewis explored the billowing falls. It was the first time white men had known the great river was broken by these curtains of water. Undisturbed by human beings, the region teemed with wildlife. The Americans had entered a kind of No Man's Land, midway between the hunting grounds of the plains Indians and the dwelling place of the mysterious mountain tribes.

A grizzly was wounded by Lewis, but the angered beast pursued him into the water, where he was nearly swept into the whirlpool formed by the falls. Later in the same day he was chased by a mountain lion, which he described in his notebook as "an animal of the tiger kind." Before sundown, buffalo trampled his knapsack and he barely escaped being bitten by the biggest rattlesnake he ever had seen.

"All nature seems in league against me," he complained that night to Clark in camp.

The portage around the Great Falls was stubborn and agonizing. Wagons had to be built of cottonwood to haul the boats and supplies. Circular sections from logs formed the crude wheels. The men's moccasins were torn to pieces by prickly pear as they shoved the clumsy carts up the steep slopes. Everyone had to take a turn at pushing. Lewis and Clark joined in the task. Only little Pompey, snugly strapped to his mother's back, was spared the ordeal. Scannon, the Newfoundland dog, licked at sore paws.

Above the falls, the party once more rowed and paddled on the Missouri. How good it felt to be in the boats again! Rowing did not seem tiresome now. But the river was narrowing. The dark mountains were closing in.

Suddenly the Missouri split into three separate rivers. Because they all were equal in size, Lewis could not decide which was the main Missouri. So he gave each of the rivers a new name. One was named for Albert Gallatin, the Secretary of the United States Treasury, and the middle fork for James Madison, who was Secretary of State. The third was named for "that illustrious person, Mr. Thomas Jefferson."

Which river to follow? In such a situation Lewis relied on a hunch. He pointed up the rushing torrent he had just named for his great hero. They paddled into the mouth of the Jefferson River.

A few days later Lewis was certain he had made the right choice. Sacajawea, who had been born a Shoshone, pointed excitedly to rounded rocks above loamy red banks.

"My people! My people!" she shouted triumphantly, in some of the few words of English she had learned.

Charbonneau explained that the Shoshones had come to this spot to collect crimson clay for war paint. They called the rounded stones "the Beaverhead Rocks," for they resembled a crouching beaver. Everyone in the expedition crowded around and listened carefully as Charbonneau talked. The heavy loads of ammunition and food and trade goods could be hauled over these lofty mountains only by horses. And horses had to be gotten from the Shoshones.

Lewis and Clark were tracking the Missouri River system to its source. Soon they would have to abandon the canoes as they had left behind the keel boat long before. With each mile, the Jefferson funneled more closely between the cliffs.

But how much could the party carry on foot across the Rockies? Their remaining supplies weighed at least four tons: 8,000 pounds. Yet could the thirty-four adults haul even a hundred pounds apiece up the steep slopes of this rugged region?

Dared they part with more than half their equipment? What could they do without? They relied on the rifles and ammunition for food. And without beads and mirrors and bolts of cloth, could they trade and make peace with the Indians who must dwell on the shores of the Western Ocean?

"Horses we must have," Lewis said with grim earnestness in the dark of a riverside encampment. "Without horses we shall leave our bones in these mountains."

But how much time remained to them? It

was only August 10—still midsummer. Yet the ink in Ordway's quill pen had been frozen when he tried to write in the frosty dawn. This was a bad sign. On the prairie, August had been a month of choking heat. But now they were high in the Rockies. They had to be across the endless ridges before snow fell. There could be no retreat for them if they were trapped in these terrible canyons by the blizzards of autumn and winter.

As he rolled in his blankets that night, Ordway wondered for the first time in many months where their British rivals were. Lewis had told his men that the President wanted them to claim for the United States all the vast area between Louisiana Territory and the mouth of "the Great River Oregon." These were the secret orders.

But would the Americans be there first? What if the Union Jack of Great Britain already waved in the salt breezes of that prized and lonely shore? Ordway tossed uneasily on the hard ground, and his dreams were troubled as he thought what this could mean to his beloved country.

6

The Search for the Shoshones

SLOSH! SLOSH! SLOSH!

The Jefferson River nipped at men's legs with icy fangs. Glaciers and snowfields fed this swift stream, which now had become too rapid and shallow to navigate.

Paddles would not breast the current. With people on the thwarts, the boats rode so low in the water that the hulls were in danger of being ripped open by the ugly saber-toothed rocks which lay in the riverbottom.

The men had to tumble overboard and wade through water, dragging the boats with ropes tied around their waists. Every few minutes someone was swept off balance and drenched from head to toe in the cold river. Boils and sores began to appear on the skin of the explorers. Clark had a large, swollen carbuncle on his ankle which he could not even bear to touch. Moccasins came apart in the rushing water and feet bled from the sharp stones. Blankets were stitched into new footgear.

Worst of all, the rock walls of the canyon came down to the river so sharply that the men could not hike on the shore and pull the boats. There was no place to walk. This was why they had to take to the water. They were lucky if they found a small beach or sand bar on which to camp at night. In the longest of the boats, they carried willow branches to build up beds that would be dry.

At one of these miserable bivouacs, Lewis had confided to Clark that they were not making fast enough progress. "The river twists and turns too much," he whispered. "We travel far, but we are not moving westward with sufficient speed. We spend our failing energy moving in circles."

At the end of the next day they had splashed up the Jefferson at least another fifteen miles. Lewis looked around him at the party. The men lay exhausted on a narrow shelf of lava rock. Sacajawea gently rubbed the aching feet of her husband, Charbonneau. Not one of the travelers was dry, unless it was little Pompey. They had not shot an elk or deer for a week, and the diet of soup stock and tea failed to nourish them for this grueling work.

To add to their discomfort, the rocks of the canyon were alive with rattlesnakes. No one could put down his foot beyond the edge of the water without examining the ground closely. Death might lurk on some boulder where a man would sit. They often saw whole nests of snakes, with hundreds of serpents coiled in hideous patterns.

Because of the snakes, some men did not like to sleep ashore at nights. They preferred to nap in the boats. Private Joseph Whitehouse had not been afraid of the savage Sioux, but he said with a shudder, "Keep me from those rattlers! I get the creeps when I look at them."

Lewis climbed out of the canyon, picking

his way slowly up the dizzy crags. Once on the rim, he found he could nearly look down on the sand bar where they had camped the night before. He shook his head in discouragement and slid back down into the canyon.

"We traveled fifteen miles today," he said to Clark, "but we are barely three miles farther west than we were yesterday." And then he added: "We must find the Shoshones."

They knew the Indians had seen them. Smoke signals wafted upward in the summer sky from distant mountain peaks. Perhaps the tribesmen were warning each other of the approach of this strange expedition. And one afternoon the sharp-eyed Clark spotted moccasin tracks in a swampy place along the riverbank. The tracks were pigeon-toed, like those of an Indian, and they were still soggy.

"Shoshone!" said Clark. "And he was here within the hour."

But still they never met the Indians face to face. They felt they were being watched. Yet the watchers never appeared.

Lewis and Clark were now almost at the head of the river. The Jefferson had narrowed until it was barely more than a wide creek. And August was wearing on toward an end. With September would come the first snows. Then it would be too late to cross the Rockies.

We must remember that these men had no map, no chart, not even a compass. They scarcely knew in what country they were. Surely by now they must be beyond the borders of Louisiana Territory. Even today, when the airplane has explored every foot of land, people become lost in the Rocky Mountains. Some of these people die of starvation. Imagine the task which confronted Lewis and Clark, who had no idea of the distance or difficulties that lay between them and the

71

ocean. For all they really knew, the Rocky Mountains rolled on practically forever.

At dawn Lewis had made up his mind. "Ordway! McNeal! Drouillard!" he ordered. "Pack up."

He eyed the men intently. When they put more than one blanket apiece in their knapsacks, he made them unpack. "We travel light for ourselves," he explained. "Trade goods will be our main load." And he stuffed the sacks with all kinds of trinkets.

Lewis talked hurriedly to Sacajawea and her husband. They told him that somewhere, off ahead, was a brook that formed the source of a great river on the other side of the Shining Mountains. This, thought Sacajawea, was the Lemhi. It led down from the very crest of the mountains. She had never seen it, but she had heard her parents speak of it long ago when she had been a little girl.

The two captains shook hands somberly. "Follow the Jefferson," Lewis said to Clark. "I will find you on the river when I come back with the Shoshones, and with horses. Or I will not come back at all," he finished.

The four men—Lewis, Ordway, McNeal and Drouillard—set out overland. They climbed slopes that were almost straight up and down. They clung to cliffs. They circled marshy lakes. They pushed their way through jungles of devil's club with thorns like knife blades. At night they made a camp and left beads, a looking glass and an awl for cutting moccasins on a stick beside the fire. Then they stole away and slept in a grove down the hillside.

They heard nothing in the darkness except the faint cry of a loon, but in the morning the trinkets were gone. The Shoshones had been there! Perhaps that bird call had been a signal. They tried to follow the moccasin trail, but it trickled out on hard rocks of granite. Yet now, at least, the Indians knew they were friendly. Would enemies of the Shoshones leave marvelous presents unguarded at the campfire?

Lewis and his three companions plodded on. They ate the last of their flour and soup, but did not pause to hunt. Hunger was nothing compared to the success of the expedition. Lewis even shared his own meagre ration with the others. "I'll eat after I know how we can get out of these mountains," he explained.

They crossed a grassy meadow and trudged along the side of a clear brook. It twisted up a gorge which became steeper and steeper. Perhaps this was the last, lingering source of the Missouri River. All at once the brook ended in a bubbling spring. Far ahead, they spied the summit of a great ridge. McNeal leaped lightly across the spring.

"Thank God!" he cried. "To think that I have lived to bestride the mighty Missouri."

And so, indeed, he had. Three thousand twisting miles from St. Louis, they had tracked the vast river to its birthplace.

Still they struggled on. With Lewis in the lead, they came out onto the summit of the ridge. They gazed westward. Before them, as far as the eye could see, the mountains stretched away in an immense carpet of white snowfields and green forests. On the other side of the ridge, water was flowing in a westerly direction.

Lewis realized that they were standing on the Continental Divide, the backbone of North America.

It was a victory which Americans had

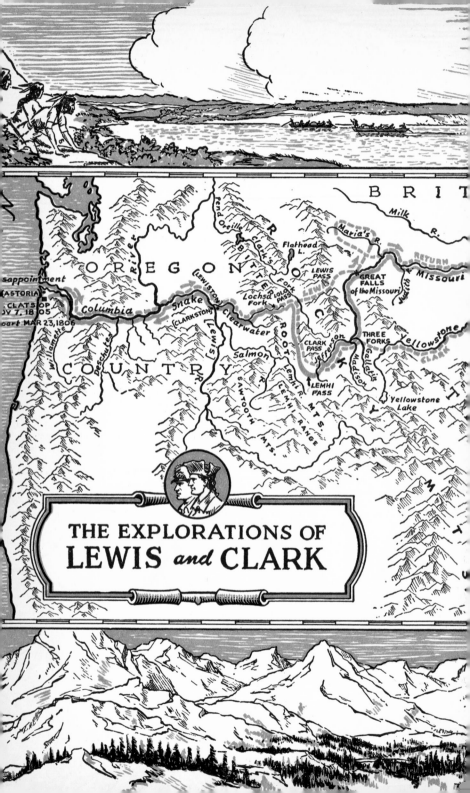

THE EXPLORATIONS OF
LEWIS and CLARK

SH TERRITORY

Martha's R.

LEWIS and CLARK
meet on return, 1806

L. Superior

FT. MANDAN
DEC. 25, 1804
winter quarters
(BISMARCK)

N

L O U I S I A N A

BLACK
HILLS

R I T O R Y

Platte R.

LEWIS & CLARK RETURN

LEWIS & CLARK

MISSOURI

Mississippi

Des Moines R.

River

Illinois

River

ST. CHARLES

ST. LOUIS

Start MAY 14, 1804
Return SEPT. 23, 1806

never before experienced. At their back, all
water eventually reached the Atlantic Ocean.
In front of them, every creek and river was
destined to join the Pacific.

With renewed strength, they plunged down
the other side of the pass. Less than a mile
along the slope, they picked up a noisy
stream. Probably this was the Lemhi, of
which Sacajawea had spoken. It gurgled
around rocks and boulders. Lewis knelt to
drink. It was cold and refreshing. The captain wrote in his diary: "I first tasted the
water of the great Columbia River."

Far off, these icy drops must unite with
"the Great River Oregon," the Columbia that
flowed to the Western Ocean.

The pass slanted gently downward. The
men hurried on. Ordway pointed to a thread-
like line in the grass of the meadow. It
was a path. Deer would not have followed

so straight a line. Indians had made this trail. Lewis was practically running. The others panted for breath as they hastened to keep up with him.

Once Drouillard, a man of the forests, made them stop as he listened with hand cupped to his ear. "Hoofs!" he exclaimed, and their excitement increased. "I hear many hoofs."

They kept walking westward, toward the sun which was descending in the sky. It was near the end of a long summer's day in the mountains. Shadows crept steadily across the wide slot of Lemhi Pass. The wildflowers waved merrily, as the winds of evening collected in the canyons far below. They seemed to be on the ceiling of the world.

Over a rise several hundred yards in front of the four white men rode sixty Indians mounted on prancing stallions and frisky ponies. War bonnets made them a picture of vivid color. The feathers bobbed to the motion of the horses. The chief in front held his spear high aloft. His followers carried bows and arrows. The chief's horse pawed the earth impatiently. It was a paint pony with red splotches against creamy hair.

The Shoshones!

7

Ponies at Last

Now the fate of the whole expedition hung by a thread.

Four white men on the roof of the continent faced sixty Shoshone braves who never before had seen anyone except other Indians.

Lewis motioned to Ordway, Drouillard and McNeal to stay behind him. He dropped his own rifle on the ground and picked up the American flag they had been carrying. It was tied to a slender pole cut from a tree of alpine fir.

Once McNeal lifted his rifle to his shoulder. Lewis angrily ordered him to put it down. "We are four against many," he said sternly. "We will make friends today or we will not leave this pass alive."

The captain advanced slowly toward the column of Indians, waving the flag as he went. One rider came forth from the main body. This was Cameahwait, chief of the Shoshones. Like Lewis, he was a young man. In the center of the meadow of buttercups and Indian paintbrush, the two at last met. The savage looked down from the pony's bare back at the secretary to the President of the United States.

The time would come when the American nation could pour westward many regiments of blue-coated cavalry, long parades of covered wagons and finally steel tracks for puffing locomotives. But now the future of the great march to the Pacific depended upon a man in tattered buckskin facing a feathered Indian on a paint pony.

Lewis knew that the Shoshones had been raided and plundered by the larger tribes of the distant plains. This was how Sacajawea had been stolen and made a slave. If the Shoshones thought Lewis were an Indian from a rival band, he would die with the chief's spear in his heart. But did they realize he was a white man? His face was burned by sun and wind. No Indian was darker.

Suddenly he breathed a prayer of thanks that he had kept on his buckskin jacket as a protection against the gnats and mosquitoes which formed a cloud wherever there was surface water in the mountains. He rolled up his sleeve. Then he held aloft the pale skin of the under part of his forearm. And he repeated over and over again words that Sacajawea had told him meant "white man":

"Tabba bone! Tabba bone!"

A murmur rippled among the Indians as they saw the white skin of the stranger. The young chief smiled gravely. Then he slid from the back of the pony and laid his spear on the ground.

"Ah hi e, ah hi e," he said.

Although Lewis did not know it at the time, in the Shoshone tongue this meant "I am much pleased." However, the chief's next action left no doubt as to his feelings. He embraced the captain. Their cheeks came together. Some of the war paint from the Indian rubbed off on the face of the explorer. They looked at each other and grinned. Lewis later claimed that he could hear, from a hundred paces away, the sighs of relief which came from Ordway, Drouillard and McNeal.

It had been a season of poor hunting. By sign language, the Shoshones now indicated that they were hungry. Fortunately, the sharpshooting Drouillard, always skillful in the woods, was able to shoot two deer. The Indians ate greedily, talking all the while about the wonderful magic of the white men.

Now they left Lemhi Pass and jogged back down to the Jefferson River to meet the rest of the party. Lewis rode bareback behind

Cameahwait on his strong pony. It was an uncomfortable ride, but Lewis thought pleasantly about the magnificent animal on which he was mounted. Such a pony could carry many supplies over the mountains to the Western Ocean!

Yells of joy sounded from the waiting camp on the Jefferson when the mounted cavalcade came into view. "Hurrah! Hurrah! They're here!" shouted Shannon, who was the first of Clark's party to see them.

Even more gleeful shouts followed a few minutes later when Sacajawea threw her arms around Cameahwait. She was the chief's long-lost sister! However, some of the happiness of this meeting was dimmed when Cameahwait told Sacajawea that all the rest of their family was dead, either from famine or from raids by the fierce Indians of the prairie.

Now followed a great council at the camp-fire. Cameahwait could not take his eyes off Clark's red hair, and into the bright locks he tied six small white shells. At the first opportunity, Clark examined the shells. His big hand trembled. The shells were hollow and curling, and had never come from a riverbed. These shells had been picked up on a seashore. Evidently the Shoshones had commerce with a tribe which lived beside the ocean. The expedition was on the right trail!

Through the interpreter, Clark asked Cameahwait a question. "Where had the shells come from?"

Cameahwait did not answer directly, but he said: "In my time I met a warrior, a Nez Percé. He told me of a great river which ran a long way toward the setting sun and finally lost itself in a great lake of water which tasted illy and made men sick to drink."

What could this lake be except the salt water of the ocean?

Lewis and Clark were more anxious than ever to be on their way. But the Shoshones drove a hard bargain for their precious horses. Cameahwait wanted only guns. With guns he could drive back the marauders from the plains. He could be master of all the Indian tribes that lived in the glow of the sun and the path of the moon. He would be the mightiest chief who ever lived.

Lewis punctured this fine dream. He had few guns to spare. Without guns, the white men would have nothing to eat. Besides, he had many medals, much brilliant cloth and jewelry in limitless quantities. All this would be the property of the Shoshones if they would provide him with horses. And through

Sacajawea and Charbonneau, he gave this message to Cameahwait:

"After we have returned to our own country, many white men will follow. They will be traders and they will be under the protection of the Great White Father. They will trade with the Shoshones through all the years to come, for as long as grass shall grow on the hills."

Cameahwait furnished a dozen sturdy ponies for the party. The white men began loading them immediately. They filled the canoes with stones and sank them in the shallow headwaters of the Jefferson. They reasoned that the boats were safer below the surface of the river than exposed to frost and snowslides and brush fires along the bank. Who knew when they would need these boats again? After all, they intended to get back to the far-off United States!

Cameahwait also gave the Americans an aged and wrinkled Indian to be their guide across the mountains. He had a long name which was hard to pronounce and spell, so Clark instantly dubbed him "Old Toby."

With the guide in the lead, they set out westward and once more crossed Lemhi Pass. At the last minute Sacajawea decided to stay with the white men instead of returning to her tribe. She told Captain Clark, who was her special friend:

"I shall never be an Indian again. The whites are my only people now. Perhaps I shall raise my son as a white man."

Old Toby's reports were not encouraging. The mountains went on for as far as Shoshones ever had journeyed. These were the Sawtooth and the Bitterroot Mountains, although to Lewis and Clark they seemed to be part of the main Rocky Mountain Range.

90

Clark and Drouillard scouted a river which rushed through a canyon a mile in depth. It was white with foam all the way. They ate pink-fleshed fish on its shores and called it the Salmon River. They also agreed it was an impossible route for people to travel. They could see long stretches of canyon where the rock walls towered straight up from the angry water.

At a place which they named Traveler's Rest Camp they repacked their equipment and tried to decide the next move. There seemed no way through the mountains. Yet they had to hurry. Already the ground had been faintly powdered with snow one morning. Some of the men would have been happy to stay in this beautiful meadow until another winter had passed. There was plenty of pine timber for a fort. The streams were bursting with fish. But Lewis scoffed at the idea.

"We have orders from Mr. Jefferson, and those orders will be carried out with all possible speed," he said.

Old Toby now pointed to a distant ridge which appeared to be split by terrifying gorges. Lewis eyed it for a long time with his telescope. Without comment, he handed the glass around a watching circle of soldiers.

"Captain," said Ordway, when it came his turn, "no man can travel that ridge."

"Sergeant," replied Lewis, "thirty-four men, a woman and a baby start traveling that ridge on the day after tomorrow."

8

Hunger on the Lolo Trail

A PONY STUMBLED ON THE SLIPPERY RIMROCK. Rain was falling, a cold and drenching rain. The man leading the animal by the tether tried to save the pony. But the rope slid through his wet fingers, scraping off the skin as it went. The pony toppled into the dark gorge with a whinnying scream of terror.

The explorers looked down into the deep abyss. From far below came a sickening thud. The animal had been carrying some of their winter clothing and the last of their skimpy supply of flour.

Yet Lewis did not see how they could struggle to the bottom of that terrible gorge and salvage the desperately-needed supplies. "What we would gain in food and clothing," he said, "we should lose in spent strength and lost time."

To give meaning to his fears about time, the rain changed to a soft, slushy snow. It soaked through moccasins and chilled the hoofs of the ponies. Old Toby often came dangerously near the edge of the narrow ridge, as he tried to peer through the blinding curtain of snow flakes.

The Shoshones had warned them that it was a poor season for game. It was even worse on this windswept ridge, high above the best pastures for elk and mule deer. And when Drouillard and York crept down to lower elevations, they still could find no targets for their guns. The approach of winter had driven the grazing animals from the uplands. More serious, there was but scant grass. The ponies were weakening beneath the heavy loads.

The party ate the final sack of corn, and Lewis sadly folded the piece of cloth. The corn, carefully rationed by Ordway, who kept track of the supplies, had lasted them from St. Louis. "Now we must truly live off the country," Lewis said.

But the country yielded no food. The men thought back hungrily to the days of fine feasts along the Missouri, when they had

eaten a whole buffalo bull every twenty-four
hours.

"My, oh my," mourned Potts. "I get ashamed
when I think how I used to throw away
buffalo ribs that were dripping with fine
chunks of meat. If only I had some of those
ribs now. I'd eat them, bones and all!"

The round Potts was scarcely recognizable.
His deerskin clothing hung on him so loosely
that he had to tighten his breeches with
twine.

Dinner that evening was service berries.
Rummaging through the underbrush to pick
this watery fruit had delayed the men several
hours. Yet the meal provided no nourishment
and they lay in their cold beds, more hungry
than ever. The skin was pulled tight on their
faces from loss of weight. Some of them looked
like walking skeletons.

One of the pony mares gave birth to a

colt. The colt provided the thirty-five adults with a slim meal, and Lewis confessed to "feeling wretched for having killed it."

But he added: "We must survive if we can. Our country expects that much of us, at least."

They dropped lines and fish hooks in Killed-Colt Creek, but a few crawfish were the only catch. By the time the shells had been cracked, barely a dozen morsels of the flaky meat remained. Lewis insisted that this food should go to the men who were the weakest. One of these was Bratton, who was ill with the flu and a hacking cough.

Lewis knew they should stop to give Bratton a chance to recover, but he said to the sick man, "If we do not get out of the mountains and off this cursed ridge, all of us soon will starve. Can you keep on going?"

Between coughing spells, the sick man

nodded in assent. Lewis had been riding a sorrel pony. Now he lifted Bratton onto the horse and took the tether himself. The others suspected that the captain was putting part of his own share of the food back into the common supply. What kept this man of iron on his feet?

Drouillard shot three pheasants and Ordway bagged a mallard duck. The food was tasty, but it did not go far among so many people. Lewis and Clark split their own portions with Scannon, a scarecrow bundle of fur and bones. "What about making a meal of the dog?" asked one of the men with hungry eyes.

Scannon had been only a last-minute purchase for twelve dollars in St. Louis. But Lewis had come to love his dog, and he scowled darkly at the soldier who had suggested that Scannon might be eaten.

"Over my dead body," said the captain. The suggestion was heard no more.

The next night a lean and daring timber wolf, made reckless by the absence of game, snapped at one of the sleeping men. Drouillard's pistol barked in the dull glow of the fire. The meat was tough and stringy, but it was meat and they made better time that day.

Yet this meant only a few miles. The ridge was choked with fallen timber. Sometimes these heavy logs had to be pushed away before the ponies could get through. The patient animals had no energy. They were forced to graze on leaves from occasional clumps of underbrush. This was not the food they required. They needed to roam in pastures with grass so high that it would tickle their bellies.

Several times Lewis wondered if they could escape from the bleak ridge. But Old Toby pointed below. In the canyon they heard the

100

dull boom of the great Lochsa Fork of the Clearwater River. No trail led down that sheer wall. Nor was there a path along the river, which was pitted with rapids. They stayed on the ridge, and the men took turns at hacking through the windfalls of dead trees.

On their hungriest night of all, dinner amounted to a quart of smelly bear's oil and the tallow melted from twenty candles. Lewis made them eat, although some could not keep down this miserable fare. "You may die if you eat," he said. "You will surely die if you don't."

Sacajawea, hollow of cheek and neck, translated this for Old Toby. The aged Indian nodded his head gravely. "White chief speak truth," he said. And Old Toby eagerly helped himself to another serving of tallow. Lewis thought that he probably enjoyed it.

Yet now the end seemed near. Clark had wrenched his hip. Lewis was staggering. Brat-

101

ton had not recovered. His cough still kept them awake at night. The ponies could barely carry a man. Their strength was fading, too. The legs of man and beast trembled as they crept along a narrow ledge which circled a cliff at least a thousand feet high. The horses' loads overhung thin air. Frost on the ledge added to the peril.

But the ridge was sloping downward. Perhaps they would get free of their mountain prison, after all! Each mile took the party closer to the river—the river which once had been so far below. Old Toby pointed dramatically. Meadows showed ahead, and they were meadows in which grass grew to the height of a pony's belly! One or two of the soldiers broke into a frenzied run.

The Clearwater was widening. No longer could they hear the thunder of rapids and falls. The river was broad and quiet. The scrubby timber of the ridge was giving way to stately pine trees. These trees had rough orange-colored bark that looked like the wrinkled skin of a crocodile. Off to the westward lay only low green hills.

They had crossed the Rockies.

Now the tireless Lewis collapsed and slept the clock around in his blankets beside the Clearwater River. His legs buckled under him when he tried to walk, and he had to return to his bed. Friendly Nez Percé tribesmen brought roots which tasted like sweet potatoes and salmon dripping with rich oil. The soldiers broiled the fish over the campfire and ate their fill. Some became deathly sick from stuffing themselves so soon after the long siege of starvation. Clark handed out Dr. Rush's pills to the sufferers.

While Lewis regained his health, the men felled pine trees to make canoes and paddles.

The wood dripped with pitch. It would make watertight vessels. Five long boats, riding deep in the river, could carry all of them and their few remaining supplies.

They planned to heap Old Toby with presents. Lewis even wanted to give him one of the President Jefferson medals, usually reserved for chiefs. He definitely would get a gun. But in the night Old Toby stole off silently. He was never seen by them again. A Nez Percé fisherman thought he had glimpsed the ancient Indian starting back up to the fearful ridge.

Tears filled Lewis' eyes. He was sure Old Toby would never survive that cheerless, windswept wilderness. By now snow would be falling steadily in the mountains. Lewis thought of dispatching a Nez Percé horseman after the guide, but Clark believed it was too late. Old Toby would think he was being pursued, and would hide in the forests.

Yet perhaps Old Toby did not die before he returned to his Shoshone tribesmen. He had never been able to pronounce the name of Lewis, whom he spoke of as "Lou Lou." As years went by, the route along the lofty ridge came to be known by the Shoshones as the Lolo Trail.

Where else did the name come from except out of Old Toby's "Lou Lou" for Lewis? No other origin seems possible.

Seventy years after the crossing by Lewis and Clark, an officer who had fought through the Civil War and who had lost an arm at the Battle of Fair Oaks led the 2nd United States Cavalry over the Lolo Trail. "I am convinced," General Oliver O. Howard reported to the War Department, "that the Lolo Trail must be the most terrible trail on all the continent of North America."

This was the trail that Lewis and Clark had blazed in September of 1805 without map or chart, but only Old Toby's pointing forearm to guide them.

9

"Ocean in View"

FOR THE FIRST TIME SINCE THEY HAD LEFT ST.
Louis nearly a year and a half before, they were
journeying downhill by water.

It was a new and light-hearted experience.
The five canoes raced each other until a sudden

eddy ended the foolish business. The boat under Sergeant Gass' direction got out of control and shipped so much water that it sank. Gass could not swim, and Cruzat had to leap in and save him from drowning. He came up gasping for air. Part of the baggage was lost, including gun powder they could scarcely spare.

"If ever again I cross the North American continent, it will be only with men who can swim," sputtered Clark, who was angry over the delay. It was one of the few occasions that he lost his temper.

"We'd better complete this crossing of North America, my friend, before we plan the next one," Lewis wryly reminded him.

The damaged boat was patched with pine pitch, and the voyage continued. Soon the Clearwater merged with another river, which was twice as broad as the Clearwater. They measured its width—1,240 feet, nearly a quarter

of a mile. Its water was apple-green in color,
and it was the biggest river they had seen on
their travels except the Missouri. Clark named
it the Lewis River over the protests of his
companion.

Yet this name has not endured. The stream
today is the Snake River, both because of its
winding course and because of the Snake Indians, who lived on its banks. However, one of
the largest communities along the Snake River
is Lewiston, Idaho, and on the opposite shore
is Clarkston, in the state of Washington.

But the states of Washington and Idaho were
not even dreamed of when Lewis and Clark
sped down the wide stream. What realm was
this? Louisiana Territory had long since been
passed. Which nation owned this vast and limitless wilderness, where a king's ransom in beaver
furs lurked at the head of every mountain
waterway?

Did it belong to Spain, to France, to England, to Russia, or to the United States?

Perhaps the frontiersmen would know when at last they stood on the shores of the Western Ocean. *If they reached the ocean!*

For the first time in many months they were well fed. The river was alive with salmon. It was early October. Although Lewis and Clark had no knowledge of the habits of this great food fish, it was the period when the autumn run swam upstream to lay their eggs. The men marveled at the abundance of the salmon. Some of the fish weighed a hundred pounds. The Indians thought that the salmon laid eggs in the very creeks where they had been born, but this seemed hard to believe.

Indians visited all the camps of the explorers along the Snake. They expressed wonder at the thick beards of men like Gass and Thompson. Other white men were smooth-shaven. Lewis,

Ordway and Shannon tried to use their open-bladed razors every day. However, this became increasingly difficult as razors dulled or were nicked to pieces. We must not forget that 4,000 miles of weary travel lay between these men and the nearest prescription shop, as drug stores were known in those days.

Private John Collins traded a piece of blue ribbon to a Nez Percé squaw for a bundle of camas roots. These came from a plant of the hyacinth family and the natives ate them daily. Collins boiled down the camas roots and made a brew which tasted like beer.

"I wouldn't give a Continental dollar for a rain-barrel full of this stuff back in Pittsburgh," said Pryor, "but it's sure welcome for a change out here."

They drank Collins' brew, ate salmon steaks as thick as oar handles, and followed it all with cups of steaming hot tea. Cruzat took out his fiddle. Such a feast called for music. Gass, who once had drawn an Army pay voucher signed by General Washington, led them in *Yankee Doodle*. A heron flapped away clumsily in fright as the voices of the homesick soldiers rose in the autumn air:

"Father and I went down to camp along with
     Captain Gooding,
And there we saw the men and boys as thick as
     Hasty Pudding.
Yankee Doodle keep it up, Yankee Doodle dandy.
Mind the music and the step, and with the girls
     be handy. . . ."

A band of roving Yakimas listened intently. The Indians had songs and chants of their own, but they never before had heard a violin. Cruzat's instrument had only two frayed strings, yet it produced a sound which fascinated the Yakimas. They insisted that he play the tune over and over again. In fact, the Indians were willing to part with many camas roots just for

another encore of *Yankee Doodle*. The squaws kept time with bare brown feet.

October was half gone when the frontiersmen came upon a huge river pouring out of the North. It was twice the width of the Snake, just as the Snake had doubled the width of the Clearwater. It was also deep beyond description, deeper even than the Mississippi, in Clark's earnest opinion.

Surely this must be "the Great River Oregon," which Americans had dreamed of exploring long before the Revolutionary War. Major Robert Rogers, organizer of the famous Rogers' Rangers, had written of "the Great River Oregon," which drained the barren lands of the sub-Arctic southward in the direction of California.

Jefferson thought this must be the Columbia River. In the year 1792 a Boston sea captain named Robert Gray had anchored his brig off the breakers at the mouth of a great river flowing into the Pacific Ocean. The river did not appear on his sketchy and incomplete charts, so he gave it a name. His vessel was the *Columbia,* and this was what he named the river.

If the so-called "Great River Oregon" flowed to the sea, it undoubtedly was the Columbia. And now Lewis and Clark were about to unlock this mystery of the North American continent.

The new river had swallowed up the Snake as a man might swallow a dipper of water. Now the combined torrents surged westward. The explorers came to rapids which dashed on for many miles. The pine-log canoes were too heavy and awkward for the men to carry on land. Instead, they had to make a run for it through the rapids.

Lewis rejoiced that the party included Cruzat and Drouillard. The French-Canadians were born rivermen. This was why they called themselves *voyageurs*. They made a profession of voyaging through rough water. Where the river billowed into mounds of spray that looked like haystacks, Cruzat would study the surface for an hour before he led the boats down. In his memory, each rock and riffle had been charted.

"Peter," said Lewis, "let me know whenever you do not want to go first through these mad stretches of the river. It is not fair that one man should take most of the risks."

"You have done me, Peter Cruzat, the great favor, *Monsieur le capitaine*," replied Cruzat. "How you say? I would not miss for the world. Is that right?"

Sacajawea also served them well. As the party leaped ashore, many of the fish-eating

"you've fought with artillery. Put your ear to the ground. Do you hear cannon?"

Ordway lay with his face against the damp earth. "Too steady for artillery, captain," he said with muffled voice.

The two men looked at each other steadily. The same thought came to both of them at once. The ocean!

Lewis put a finger to his lips in caution. "Not a word to the others," he said. "A false alarm would be very bad. The men are wondering now how long this journey must be."

Ordway nodded in agreement.

Soon it would be two years that the party had been gone from civilization. There had been many emergencies and much suffering. These hardships were not yet over. Yet always the goal was kept foremost in mind. That goal was the ocean which broke on the western rim of North America, on the shore where the flag of the United States had never flown.

Some of the men were beginning to fear that there was no such ocean. A few even had hinted that the party should turn back. What if they traveled so far that they ran out of enough ammunition and trade goods to make possible a safe return through Indian country?

Fog in heavy shrouds cloaked the river a week after they had passed the island with the burned trees. From the fifth canoe, the first boat was barely visible. It was a raw day. The tang of salt was in the air. Several of the men had quickly spat out water dipped from the river.

"Salt!" they exclaimed.

All at last realized that the destination was near.

Around noon the fog lifted slightly and framed the river. The explorers seemed to be paddling through a long corridor. Now and then a salmon broke the surface of the water with wet and arching back. The men put down the paddles and let the boats bob gently on the waves.

From the capes and headlands, the fog continued to clear. It rose like a curtain on some great stage. Streaks of sunlight shone through the mist. The men shaded their eyes and peered steadily westward.

And there it was, breaking in white-capped glory beyond the bar—the Western Ocean, the blue Pacific! The surf heaved in frothy crests. Spray was tossed by the wind. Back of the breakers, the water rolled in rippling swells.

In the notebook dated November 7, 1805, Clark scrawled: "Ocean in view! Oh the joy! We are in view of the ocean, that great Pacific Ocean we have been so long anxious to see!"

The captain with red hair and merry face had never been so excited before.

For the first time in history, Americans had crossed the continent which they one day would inhabit from coast to coast.

10

Winter on the Pacific Coast

It was a wild and lonely seacoast. Yet for these travel-weary explorers it had all the lure of a tropical isle. They had fulfilled the mission on which they had been sent by President Jefferson. Potts, always enthusiastic, kissed the wet ground in glee.

"We're here!" he shouted triumphantly. "We're here!"

More important still, there was not a sign of any other habitation by white men. When Lewis brought ashore from the first canoe the biggest of their American flags, it flew alone in the stiff breeze from the ocean. No other flag waved nearby to challenge it.

In the past, a few ships had anchored in the mouth of this mighty river. Lewis and Clark learned that fact when they stopped at Indian villages near the coast. Some of the families of the Clatsop tribe had frying pans, powder flasks, copper kettles and various pieces of sailors' uniforms. This meant that the Indians had traded with men on ships—perhaps with Captain Gray and his crew on the *Columbia,* or with the British frigate *H. M. S. Discovery,* commanded by Captain George Vancouver.

But these adventurers had come only by sea.

They had not established themselves on land. They arrived and departed, and a few articles left in Indian huts were the only trace of their visit.

After Lewis and Clark had scoured the sandy beaches for many miles, the two leaders realized that they were definitely the first white men to reach the mouth of the Columbia from the interior of the continent. On the other side of each timbered headland, they braced themselves to see a British fort. But the coast was vacant. America's claim to the vast valley of the Columbia seemed secure.

"I guess our English friends found the mountains tough, too," commented Clark.

But now the explorers had to return to the far-off United States with all their maps and drawings and stuffed animals. The biggest bundles in their baggage were full of various hoofs and claws, dried ferns and rocks that seemed to be streaked with minerals. How else could Thomas Jefferson know of their discoveries?

A stormy winter was in prospect. As the days of November passed, the wind blew in fitful gales across the choppy bar where the Columbia joined the Pacific.

Should they camp for the winter on the north or the south shore of the river? They paddled back and forth in the ungainly pine-log canoes. This was a dangerous voyage in the watery troughs which rolled in from the ocean. The mouth of the Columbia is more than seven miles wide.

Many of the men were sea-sick. "I don't care where we camp," moaned John Colter, who never before had seen salt water. "But let's just camp somewhere on dry land."

Lewis had been told by the Indians that deer were more numerous on the north shore.

Elk abounded on the south bank. Deer tasted better to eat, but elk hide was stronger and more durable. They needed good food, yet they also needed new clothing. Their garments were in shreds. Even more serious, none of them had a pair of moccasins which shed water any longer.

"Let's vote on the question," Lewis proposed.

Sixty-five years were to pass before Article XV would be added to the Federal Constitution, protecting the right to vote regardless of a person's race or color. For this reason it is interesting to learn that the stalwart Negro, York, was handed a ballot along with the rest. No one thought to deny him a vote. Sacajawea also was allowed to take part. With Charbonneau's help, she even made a little speech.

"South side best," said she. "More wappatos on south side."

"Good for Janey," chimed in Clark, using

his own private name for Sacajawea. He, too, enjoyed eating the wappato, a wild root which had a flavor similar to that of an Irish potato.

The south shore got a big majority of the votes. Thus it was that the first settlement by Americans on the Pacific Coast came to be located in the future state of Oregon rather than across the Columbia River, where the state of Washington one day would be.

They selected a site on high ground above the waves and began splitting fir and cedar logs. Axes bit into wood during every daylight hour. The rain fell constantly. The wind blew down their buffalo-skin tents. Bedding was soggy. This gave speed to the building of Fort Clatsop. All of them ached to get under shelter. The damp climate brought out rheumatism in arm and leg joints. Bratton still coughed most of the time. Dr. Rush's medicine seemed to have no effect. Perhaps he was coming down with tuberculosis.

In the bark of a tall fir tree overlooking the fort, Clark carefully carved a record of the journey:

WM. CLARK DECEMBER 3D 1805
BY LAND FROM THE U. STATES
IN 1804 & 5.

It comes as a shock to us to realize that these men did not consider themselves in the United States. They had traveled 4,100 miles since leaving St. Louis. They looked upon the United States as being that far away—farther than London is from New York! Lewis and Clark regarded Oregon as part of a foreign land. It was only a hope and a prayer that this land some time would be part of the United States.

And would they ever get back to the United States?

"All our trade goods could be tied up in a couple of big handkerchiefs," Lewis wrote in his notebook.

They were running out of things to barter with the Indians. The men ripped brass buttons off their folded Army jackets to use in hiring help for the construction of Fort Clatsop. There was only enough tobacco left for a smoke apiece on Christmas Day. Then it would be gone.

Lewis would not let the soldiers give out presents generously to the coastal tribes. These eaters of fish and roots were not warlike Indians. "We shall save the few trade goods we have left," Lewis said, "for the trip across the plains. We may really need them."

All the men understood exactly what he meant. Between them and St. Louis were the lands of the savage Sioux and the fierce Blackfeet. Presents might be extremely necessary to buy a peaceful passage through the hunting grounds of these hard-riding warriors of the prairie.

On December 25, 1805, the explorers moved into Fort Clatsop. "What finer Christmas gift than to be warm and dry?" happily asked George Shannon, who had just celebrated his nineteenth birthday by bringing down a great elk in a swamp near the river's mouth.

The fanciest present of all was given by Sacajawea to her favorite, Captain Clark. On the table in front of him, she piled twenty-four glistening pelts of white ermine. They had been carried in her belongings from Fort Mandan. "Ho, Janey! What a present!" cried Clark. The men crowded around to feel the soft fur.

Platters of roasted elk meat dotted the boards. The men filled their pipes with the last of the tobacco and puffed away in comfort. That evening Cruzat played his worn fiddle.

They sang Christmas carols which had come from the Old World. Even little Pompey woke up. Although he was now nearly a year old, he was still carried on his mother's back. His yells mingled with the chanting voices of the soldiers.

Meriwether Lewis smoked his pipe and thought of his great friend in the White House. What treasures he would be able to describe to Mr. Jefferson! This land was rich beyond telling.

From shore to shore, the Columbia River was bursting with salmon. Surely this one river had more fish than all the fisheries of New England. A Maine salmon weighed ten pounds. Those of the Columbia weighed ninety and a hundred pounds.

On the Columbia's wooded banks, elk grazed and deer foraged. These were huge, tawny deer with sleek sides, the Columbian blacktails. And never before had Americans looked up at such trees. "They are the straightest and most beautiful logs I ever have seen," scribbled Lewis. "They would deck our finest clipper ship or form the spire of the most magnificent church."

He was referring to the lofty firs which mantled every hillside. Some of these trees, he estimated, were at least 220 feet high. Think of what an industry in lumber this might make some day!

Everyone was busy during the long winter on that rainy coast. York and Gass, the brawniest of the men, chopped wood to keep the fires going. This was the most rugged work of all. The dripping chunks of fir were often as heavy as iron. Drouillard and Field hunted in the forests for elk. Ordway and Colter and Sacajawea fashioned moccasins with awls. They made 338 pairs!

Clark looked at the mighty heap of footgear, and he thought of the endless miles of mountains between them and home. "We'll need all these moccasins before we see St. Louis again," he said.

The soldiers did not have to ask what he was talking about. They knew all too well. In fact, the memory of the terrible mountain trails caused them to keep a lookout on the highest headland above the ocean. A few ships had put into the mouth of the Columbia once. This could happen again. How much easier it would be to journey back to the United States in the fo'c'sle of a frigate than to struggle across the Rockies and the plains!

But no sail was sighted from Cape Disappointment. No vessel answered their signal fire. Not a brig dotted the lonely expanse of sea. It began to be evident that they would have to return over the same grueling route by which they had come. The preparations began early.

Elk meat was smoked and dried. Salmon was preserved by the same method. Many of the guns did not work properly. Shields, the blacksmith, fashioned new gun parts at his forge. Everyone cut himself fresh garments of elk hide. Powder flasks were opened to make sure the ammunition was dry. A huge supply of roots and berries was stowed in the sacks which once had held flour and corn.

Ordway discovered that the inner bark of red willow trees could be mashed up and smoked in their empty pipes. It did not take the place of tobacco, but the aroma was pleasant.

Lewis dipped into his few remaining trade goods and bought cone-shaped hats which the Indians wove from cedar bark. This was a novelty and the soldiers thought they looked very dashing, indeed.

Ordway, who was descended from the Pilgrim Fathers, gazed at himself in the mirror. "This hat of bark makes me resemble my own ancestors!" he said to his fellow sergeant, Pryor.

As the time drew near to abandon Fort Clatsop, Lewis wrote far into the night by the glow of the fire in his cabin. Who knew what might befall them on the long journey homeward? Yet a record had to be left somewhere telling what they had done.

Lewis was penning a statement about the expedition. This statement told that the soldiers and their officers had been "sent out by the government of the United States in May, 1804, to explore the interior of the continent of North America by way of the Missouri and Columbia Rivers."

Their route was described and each man signed the statement. Those who could not write their names put down an "X".

Lewis added a note requesting that the statement be made known to the world if it ever came into the hands of a "civilized person."

The captain made extra copies of the statement until his hand had writer's cramp. One copy was posted inside his cabin at Fort Clatsop. Another was nailed up in the quarters occupied by the private soldiers. Several copies were given to friendly old Chief Comowool of the coastal tribes. He had danced many times to Cruzat's music, and had brought the white men gifts of fish and roots. The chief promised to guard the papers with his life.

At one o'clock on the afternoon of March 23, 1806, the party trudged out of Fort Clatsop. They waved in farewell to the aged chief, whom Lewis had made the official new owner of the fort.

Within a few weeks Comowool would turn over a copy of the statement to Samuel Hill,

master of the brig *Lydia,* from Boston. By only
nineteen days did Lewis and Clark miss a boat
ride back to the United States.

Fort Clatsop had been their shelter. It had
protected them from storm and gale. Their
labor and toil had erected its log walls. It was
the first building Americans ever had put up
on the shores of the Pacific Ocean. In a way,
it was home for these frontiersmen who had
been gone so long from homes of their own.

When they last saw Fort Clatsop Chief
Comowool was standing proudly in front of
the gate. On his chest gleamed a medal which
bore a carved likeness of the Great White
Father, Thomas Jefferson.

11

Bloodshed on the Plains

Summer had come again to the green and peaceful place which Lewis and Clark called "Traveler's Rest Camp."

The grass in the meadows had never been so thick and high. A moose with spreading

139

antlers nibbled at the juicy forage. Gray squir-
rels scampered up and down the tree trunks.
Bluebells and johnny-jump-ups and other wildflowers brightened the scene with color.

On the limb of a quacking aspen, a bluejay
chattered noisily as it scolded a pair of furry
beavers. These beavers were gnawing at pine
trees along the rippling creek. Already they
had toppled two trees across the stream. By
winter the beavers hoped to have the creek
blocked with a dam, so that they might move
into a pond home.

All the other sounds of the mountains in
summer could be heard, too. A thrush sang
its clear song. Several bandtailed pigeons
flapped from branch to branch with fluttering
wings. In the sky a V-shaped wedge of Cana-
dian geese flew north. A mountain lion with
twitching tail stalked along the edge of the
meadow. The beavers splashed into the safety

of the water. The bluejay scolded more loudly than ever.

The moose looked up suspiciously, then put its clumsy nose back into the grass. The moose knew the mountain lion would never tempt those antlers which glistened like a bundle of swords.

Hark! What was that, far off in the range? It was a new sound which the wild creatures of Traveler's Rest Camp could scarcely remember.

Down the long slope from the ridge came the clatter of many pony hoofs. Bluejay and thrush listened to the babble of men's voices. These were not sing-song Indian voices. This was a strange tongue that the birds and animals of the green meadow had heard only once before. The white men had returned.

The mountain lion bounded off. Even the moose sensed danger and slipped back into the dark forests, pushing aside underbrush and small trees as it went.

The explorers slumped down wearily in the grass. Ordway mopped sweat from his forehead. "Well," he said to Pryor, "the ridge wasn't as bad as last fall. I'll admit that. But I hope I never see that ridge again if I live until the year 1900."

Pryor dipped a cloth in the cold creek and wiped his face, which was streaked with dirt. "That goes for me, too," he said with feeling.

The men of Lewis and Clark had come up the Columbia and over Lolo Pass, repeating the trail of the year before.

With almost the last of their trade goods, they had paid the smiling Nez Percé along the Clearwater for taking care of the ponies through the long winter. But the men of the expedition saw their friend Cameahwait no more. The Shoshones were a wandering tribe, and they had melted back into the ravines and canyons. Sacajawea had hoped for another reunion with her brother, but it was not to be.

And now Lewis and Clark called the most serious council meeting they ever had held. The campfire that night was ringed with solemn faces. The three sergeants, Ordway and Gass and Pryor, leaned silently against hemlock trees just outside the glow of light. Lewis stood beside the fire, a paper in his hand. Clark stood beside him, with folded arms.

"Men," began Lewis, "I hold here the map I am preparing for President Jefferson. I don't know whether any other people ever will follow our trail into these fastnesses. But right now this map wouldn't help them very much. Too much of it is completely blank."

Lewis held the map high over his head, so all the soldiers at the campfire could see it. Then he continued:

"The continent of North America is a very big place, and we have to fill in some of the white space on this map. We haven't enough gun powder and other supplies to roam all around this wild region for another year or more. But there is a way we can do the job in a hurry."

Now Lewis outlined his bold plan. He proposed to split the expedition into three separate parties. Clark would follow last year's trail as far as the headwaters of the Yellowstone. Then he would leave the trail to go down that swift stream to the Missouri. Sergeant Ordway would pick up the canoes which had been sunk in the Jefferson River. Lewis would take nine volunteers and explore the mountains off to the north, in the direction of Canada.

The party headed by Lewis would meet Ordway with the boats near White Bear Island. These two companies would voyage together down the Missouri. They would join Clark's party at the junction of the Missouri and Yellowstone Rivers.

It sounded simple. Yet there was doubt on some of the faces at the campfire. "I am not optimistic," said Sergeant Gass. In so vast and trackless a land, three small parties of white men were no larger than the head of a very small pin. How easy it might be to miss each other entirely! Of course, the Missouri River was always a thread which led back to the United States.

Lewis added a final warning:

"I think it is reasonable to say that we have been spared attack because we have been many. But Indians who would hesitate to attack thirty-three strangers might not feel the same about eight or nine. There is safety in numbers, and now we are splitting our numbers three ways. Yet there is no way of helping it. We must take the risk if we are to do our duty."

They were a somber lot in the gray dawn as they divided at Traveler's Rest Camp. All realized that the particular party headed by Lewis was moving into the greatest peril. His tiny band was entering the realm of the Blackfeet, fiercest of the tribes of the plains and foothills. In addition, this party would not be in familiar surroundings. For part of the time, at least, the parties led by Clark and Ordway would have the benefit of last year's experience.

For this reason, Lewis was taking most of the ponies. He also had picked out the fleetest ones. Lewis raised himself on the back of his pony and lifted his hand silently in farewell. Up to him came Clark's parting cry, "Good luck!"

With Gass as his principal aide, Lewis crossed the mountains at a wide gap in the Rockies which Drouillard thought should be named "Lewis and Clark Pass." They came down into a narrow valley full of buffalo. It was a sea of animals. The bellowing of the bulls sounded like thunder. The horses danced in fright, and the white men had to circle the herd cautiously. Lewis believed the little valley held 20,000 milling beasts.

Long after they had passed the great herd, Lewis saw a lone buffalo writhing in pain on the ground. The animal had a gaping wound in the shoulder. From the wound protruded an arrow. Blackfeet! At the crest of a low hill, they met eight mounted Indians.

With Drouillard acting as interpreter, a pow-wow was held. Lewis was disturbed to notice that these Indians accepted with stony expressions his gifts of handkerchiefs, a flag and a medal. The Blackfeet also wanted to camp with them at night. A few of the white men were afraid, but Lewis replied tersely,

"Mr. Jefferson wants to know about these people. We shall find out."

And that night they did.

Drouillard, a wilderness man who slept as lightly as a cat, woke to find his rifle being slipped away by one of the Blackfeet. "Let go my gun!" he shouted.

Reuben Fields, one of the Kentucky mountaineers, was out of his blanket in a flash. He leaped on the Indian with his hunting knife. The blade was driven into the Indian's naked back. The Blackfoot slid to earth, dead.

The camp was suddenly alive. Another Blackfoot had taken Lewis' pistol from his belt while he slept. Drouillard drew a bead on the thief in the bright prairie moonlight, but Lewis knocked up his gun. "We're under orders to avoid bloodshed if possible," he cautioned.

Drouillard looked at his captain angrily. "It is not possible with these people," he answered.

But Lewis had to go back on his own orders. Another Blackfoot was trying to stampede the expedition's tethered ponies. This would be a calamity—to be in the heart of hostile country without horses. Lewis shot the Indian in the stomach. Before he died, the Blackfoot returned a shot that whisked off Lewis' fur hat. Evidently other guns had been stolen that night.

"Mount and ride!" cried Lewis.

The six remaining Indians were disappearing over a hump of ground. The fight had not gone as they planned. Their strategy apparently had been to slip away the guns of all the white men in their sleep. Then the Indians would have been masters of the situation. Only Drouillard's alertness had avoided a disaster.

The white men ran for the ponies. Lewis looked back at the shambles of their camp. He stooped to pick up the American flag he had given the Blackfeet in friendship the evening before. On the chest of one of the slain braves was the medal with the President's image.

Lewis was going to rip it off the body, then hesitated. No, he would leave the medal with its inscription "United States of America." The Blackfeet had started the bloody fight. It was best that this savage tribe know the soldiers of the Great White Father were men whose wrath was to be feared.

Yet now the white men had to get out of the domain of the Blackfeet, and in a hurry.

The Indians might return with the whole tribe. In that case, Lewis and his little band would be massacred. Furthermore, the other two parties of the expedition could know nothing of this encounter. But smoke signals might pass the message among the Blackfeet in a few days. The groups led by Clark and Ordway would be in peril of ambush. They had to be warned.

"We must ride and ride hard," Lewis said.

They made 121 miles before evening of the next day. The ponies gasped for breath. "On, Old Timer," Lewis whispered to his horse. A few lumps of sugar remained in the bottom of one of their sacks. The men had saved the sugar for a feast when they finally would be on the Missouri again. Now it went to the faithful ponies, to rally their failing strength.

Often the white men looked back over the horizon. Once they thought they saw clouds of dust. They rode all night, picking their way in the darkness among mounds of sleeping buffaloes. They killed a buffalo calf with a knife, to avoid the noise of a shot. The flesh was eaten nearly raw. A long delay to roast the meat would cost them their scalps.

The ponies were staggering when at last the

party led by by Lewis reached the river. They were overjoyed to find the dependable Ordway at the rendezvous with the canoes. Lewis put an arm around his pony's head affectionately. "Goodbye, Old Timer," he said. "I hope some good Indian gets you."

They dropped down the bank and into the boats. The ponies were left on the riverbank grazing contentedly.

Lewis sat gloomily in the canoe. Even a happy meeting with Clark downstream from the mouth of the Yellowstone did not raise his spirits. After more than 6,000 miles of peaceful travel, Indian blood had been shed. Lewis drew from the waterproof packet near his heart the letter of instruction handed him by the President. He read one sentence many times:

"In all your relations with the natives, treat them in a most friendly manner."

Had he violated Mr. Jefferson's orders? The others assured him over and over again that he had not. After all, he had only protected their lives. He could not carry out any orders from Mr. Jefferson if he had a Blackfoot spear in his breast. Yet Lewis worried that a war between red men and white had been started in the West which might last for a hundred years.

12

Back to the United States

Disbelief was written all over the friendly face of Henry Delaunay, French trader from St. Louis.

"Lewis and Clark! Lewis and Clark!" he kept repeating. "They're slaves in the Mexican silver mines. They were captured on the Colorado River by the Spanish cut-throats. *Le bon Dieu,* gentlemen, you can't be Lewis and Clark!"

"But we are!" shouted Lewis and Clark in one breath.

Paddling swiftly downstream on the Missouri, the party was commencing to meet white men. They had passed Fort Mandan, their home during an icy prairie winter. It was now a heap of charred ruins, burned in a sweeping grass fire.

Lewis thought of another fort, far away. "I wonder if old Chief Comowool is safe and sound in Fort Clatsop?" he said to himself.

Razors had long since crumbled to pieces, so Henry Delaunay saw only bearded men in the boats opposite his own. When he finally believed this was the Lewis and Clark expedition, he embraced the captains joyously.

The Frenchman had a few bottles of champagne. This was passed around and toasts drunk. Better still, Delaunay could spare a barrel of flour. That night they ate pancakes until no one could rise to his feet. Potts stopped at fifty-two! They had lived on meat and fish for more than a year. Now they craved things made of dough.

From Delaunay the captains learned that the expedition had long since been given up for lost. Only President Jefferson held out hope that they were still alive. His political enemies were blaming him for the deaths of all the men on the expedition.

There seemed no end to the fantastic stories being circulated throughout the United States. Some people said that Lewis and Clark were prisoners of the Spaniards. Others were sure they had been eaten by prehistoric monsters.

Still others claimed they had perished in mountains of rock salt, where there was neither food nor water.

They paddled more furiously than ever now. How glorious to confront the foes of President Jefferson with their safe return!

But Charbonneau had no desire to share in this triumph. He wanted to leave the expedition, for the plains were his home. There he would hunt and trap, and act as an interpreter for traders. Having been to the Pacific Ocean with Lewis and Clark, he would find his services in greater demand than ever. Sacajawea wept, but she would stay with her husband.

"I will bring my son to you, to be raised as a great captain," she promised Clark. Her eyes were red with tears. Charbonneau received from Lewis an order on the United States government for $500. This was his pay. Sacajawea lifted little Pompey high over her head for all to see, as the boats swept out of sight.

John Colter was next to part with his comrades. He had joined in with two trappers, who asked Colter to guide them through the valley of the Yellowstone. Although Colter was the youngest man on the expedition, he had fallen under the spell of the wilderness. He said he never wanted to see civilization again.

Farther downstream, the remaining members of the expedition hailed a boat commanded by an old Army friend of Lewis. From Captain John McClallan they learned about politics. Lewis slapped his thighs in glee when he was told that Thomas Jefferson had swept the Presidential election of 1804. McClallan couldn't even remember the name of the other candidate.

"All I know is that Mr. Jefferson got just about every electoral vote," he added.

McClallan filled the canoes with chocolate,

onions, biscuits and dried fruit. It had been a long time since the explorers had tasted these foods, and they smacked their lips over every bite. McClallan also provided them with razors, and they scraped off beards that nearly covered their broad chests.

St. Charles was now in sight. Word had been passed down the Missouri from boat to boat that Lewis and Clark were returning. The village wharf was lined with cheering people. Ordway looked for Sarah and her mother in the crowd, but did not see them.

That night the mayor of St. Charles gave a great ball. The orchestra played patriotic music. American flags were everywhere. Ordway finally found Sarah's mother, and she was his partner for a gay polka.

"When I was up on top of the Continental Divide, I thought of that wonderful glass of milk you gave me," he said

"I'll certainly tell Sarah what you said," the woman told him laughingly. "Then perhaps she may drink her milk more willingly at home."

St. Louis was just down the Missouri. The Lewis and Clark expedition arrived there on September 23, 1806. It was a holiday in the city. Everyone who could walk on foot or ride a carriage was along the riverbank to see the heroes. They landed amidst the welcoming boom of artillery, firing in salute. They had been gone two years, four months and twelve days

13

A Great Tale to Tell

LEWIS AND CLARK WERE BACK!

The tale spread slowly through the nation. In those days, there was no telegraph or telephone, and of course no radio. All the great news had to travel by mail, which went on horseback or stage coach. This meant that children in St. Louis knew the marvelous story much earlier than children in Philadelphia or Boston, or in other cities farther east.

But soon the Lewis and Clark expedition was the topic on every tongue. Some people could hardly believe the things the frontiersmen said. One newspaper in New York suggested that the country which had been explored was so wild that it probably would never be visited again.

Bears that weighed a thousand pounds and more! Mountains many times the height of the Adirondacks! A river bigger than the Missouri and full of fish! Waterfalls that disappeared in spray! Trees taller than the tallest church steeple! Buffalo as far as the eye could see!

The parents of school children in Connecticut read this column in a paper called the *Hartford Courant*:

Lewis and Clark were the first white people who ever went to that great country. There are horses without number. It is thought to be a very poor Indian who does not own 300 horses, and not an iron tool among them.

Lewis and Clark erected a log fort on the sea shore and carved their names. They have a number of curiosities. They have a stuffed wild sheep. The head and horns alone weigh over 90 pounds! It was shot on the Rocky Mountains.

The explorers were asked to repeat constantly the tale of the bighorn sheep. People's eyes bulged in wonder when they saw the head, with its great curving horns. Many refused to believe that this strange creature leaped from ledge to ledge at the very top of the highest mountain peaks.

Wherever they went, the men of the expedition were treated as heroes. Parades greeted them in many cities. Children were named in their honor. The President received the frontiersmen with open arms at the White House.

"I heard of your return with unspeakable joy," he said.

Better still, Mr. Jefferson sent a message to Congress recommending that each soldier on the expedition receive 320 acres of fine land as a bonus. Captain Lewis and Captain Clark were to get 1,500 acres apiece.

And the President ordered the War Department to give the explorers double pay for all the time they had been on the trail. And so the privates were paid ten dollars a month in gold, instead of the five they had been promised. The three sergeants, Ordway and Gass and Pryor, had their monthly wages increased from eight to sixteen dollars. In addition, each man was issued five brand new uniforms with gold braid and brass buttons.

Then Lewis remembered the comrade who could not share in these rewards. "Sir," he said to Mr. Jefferson, "I believe I should call to your attention the death of Sergeant Charles Floyd on the Missouri River."

"Well spoken," replied the President.

To Floyd's parents in Kentucky went double pay of the rank of sergeant for twenty-eight months, as well as a deed to 320 acres of rich bottom land in Louisiana Territory.

And now new maps began to appear on the walls of school rooms. All at once the blank space west of St. Louis was filled in. The children realized the vast size of the continent on which they lived. They saw for the first time the exact location of the Rocky Mountains, the Columbia River, even of the Pacific Ocean.

A famous painter in Philadelphia, Charles Willson Peale, did portraits of Meriwether Lewis and William Clark. Copies of these paintings were sent all over the country. Many hung in school rooms. Small boys played games in which they pretended to be one of the bold explorers. Garden lovers wrote to the White House for seeds of the western plants which Lewis and Clark had brought back with them.

Clark soon learned that there were some things more terrifying than the lonely plains and rugged mountains.

"I'm more scared now, darling, than when I was in Indian country," he whispered to pretty Julia Hancock. This was at a public banquet in his honor at Fincastle, Virginia. "I'd rather fight the Blackfeet than have to make a speech!"

In banks and counting houses, men of wealth studied the thick diary kept so carefully by Lewis during 8,200 miles on the trail. They at last understood the riches in furs, land, fish, timber and minerals which lay to the westward. Of course, these men knew nothing about water power, so they could not be aware of the energy lurking in the white foam of the rivers that had been traveled.

A millionaire merchant prince named John Jacob Astor wrote to the President, "I am amazed at the apparent wealth of this western domain explored by Captains Lewis and Clark."

And Mr. Jefferson replied, "I view a great, free and independent empire on the Columbia River."

When Astor received this letter he began outfitting a schooner, the *Tonquin,* to circle the Horn and establish a permanent post alongside the log stockade of Fort Clatsop. This was the beginning of the American Fur Company. Another Astor party would trek overland. In fact, all westward migration across the plains and mountains dates from the return of the Lewis and Clark expedition.

But not even President Jefferson could foresee the future of the lands which the great exploration had added to the United States. The colonies had become a continent.

Today the area explored by Lewis and Clark forms large parts of the states of Missouri, Kansas, Iowa, Nebraska, South Dakota, North Dakota, Wyoming, Montana, Idaho, Oregon and Washington. This is the bread-basket of our country.

At no other period in the history of a mighty nation was so rich and vast a land opened up all at once.

In the midst of the national celebration honoring Lewis and Clark, the brig *Lydia* put into Boston harbor from the South Seas. In the log of the *Lydia* was the statement written by Lewis, which old Chief Comowool had handed to the ship's master. And the captain of the sailing ship told people in Boston that Comowool had said Lewis and Clark were "real chiefs," the greatest chiefs the Indians of the coastal tribes had ever known.

What finally became of some of these brave men who had done so much to enrich their country?

14

The End of the Expedition

JOHN COLTER THOUGHT THE END HAD COME. HE was tied to a splintered post in a Blackfoot village. Four years of trapping beaver in the Rockies had brought him to the torture stake. His companion, the jolly Potts, lay dead in their canoe back on the Jefferson River, a dozen arrows in his body.

Colter had been captured alive.

The Indians argued about how to kill their prisoner. Colter had learned the Blackfoot language, and now he took the only desperate course open to him. He sent for the tribal chief and said he had been with the great white captains, Lewis and Clark. The chief's eyes narrowed in anger.

"The follower of such great captains is a fit test for Blackfoot bravery," said Colter. "He should not die without letting your warriors kill him in a fair fight. Think what a tale that would be to tell at Blackfoot council fires!"

The chief accepted the challenge. Completely naked, Colter was led out on the upland plain. When he was 300 yards in front of the howling tribe, he was ordered to run. At that instant, the Indians started in pursuit.

It hardly seemed a contest. The Indians wore moccasins, but Colter was bare-footed. The plain was covered with stones and prickly pear. Soon his feet were torn and bloody.

But Colter was running for life. He was young and strong. The Indians also were slowed by the assortment of weapons they carried. Soon Colter had pulled away from all the Indians except one youthful brave. This warrior was gaining on him. Each second, the white man expected to feel the barbed spear in his bare back.

Again, only one course was open to Colter. He took it.

He stopped suddenly. The surprised Indian, fooled by this trick, could not halt. He stumbled while trying to throw the heavy spear. Immediately, Colter picked up the weapon and jabbed it into the fallen Blackfoot.

He ran desperately now. He scarcely felt

pain in his bleeding feet. The Indians would be doubly anxious to avenge their tribesman. Finally, Colter came to the Jefferson River and leaped in. He swam to a little island, where some drifting logs had formed a loose raft. He came up under this raft just as the Indians reached the riverbank.

All that day and night, Colter lay naked in the icy river. By getting his nostrils up into the air space beneath the logs, he was able to breathe. Sometimes the moccasined toes of the Blackfeet were so close he feared they could hear his breathing. But at last they gave up the search. Seven days later, Colter crawled on hands and knees into Lisa's Fort, a frontier trading post.

This youngest of the men who had gone west with Lewis and Clark lived to wander into a remote valley which was polkadotted with weird springs. These springs blew hot water

told in broken English about the valiant captains she had known so long ago.

And Meriwether Lewis, the leader of the
greatest exploration in American history—what
became of him?

President Jefferson appointed Lewis to be
governor-general of all the Louisiana Territory.
But Lewis was not happy in this high position.
He longed for the woods and high mountains.
He remembered how the western slope of the
Rockies had looked on that summer's day when
he crossed the Continental Divide. No dusty
office could compare with that.

James Madison replaced Thomas Jefferson in
the White House, and Lewis slipped into a long
spell of gloom. He was often careless with official papers, and the new government complained about his reports. He decided to ride
from St. Louis to Washington, D. C., where he
would silence this criticism.

Lewis was a lonely man as he galloped along the post road. His followers on the trail were scattered. His faithful Newfoundland **dog**, Scannon, had died on the hearth.

Meriwether Lewis had never married. Yet he knew his name would be carried on. Clark's first son was Meriwether Lewis Clark. The grandson of Thomas Jefferson had been christened Meriwether Lewis Randolph. The ex-President had picked the name himself.

On the gusty night of October 10, 1809, with a lightning storm flickering in the sky, Lewis stopped at a wayside inn in Tennessee called Griner's Stand. His lieutenant had ridden back in the rain to round up several pack horses that had broken loose.

In the early morning a pistol shot woke the household. The inn-keeper found the 35-year-old explorer on the dirt floor of the bedroom with a gaping wound in his side. He died at dawn.

Jefferson, overcome with grief at his home in Virginia, believed Lewis had killed himself. But some people in Tennessee thought Lewis had been murdered. Suspicion was directed for a time at the owner of the inn. In 1849 the legislature of Tennessee decided that Lewis was shot "by the hand of an assassin." To this day his death remains a mystery.

Ordway, about to settle on his 320 acres of fertile land, visited the grave where Lewis lay buried. The sergeant wore his new uniform. It was 1st Infantry. He decided Lewis would have liked that. First Infantry had been the captain's regiment, too.

As he stood by the grave marker, Ordway thought again of the march to Oregon. He saw the captain trudging alone with the flag across the pass to meet the armed Shoshones.

He remembered the look on the captain's face when they had seen that terrible ridge above Traveler's Rest Camp, and the captain had said in a ringing voice that they would travel the ridge or die in the attempt. He recalled how the captain had dismounted in the snow and given his pony to the sick and coughing Bratton.

Ordway stood with stiff back and head held high at the place where the captain was buried. He saluted, as he had done so often before. Then he turned to walk away. The wind sighed heavily in the trees overhanging the grave.

Ordway thought for a moment that the wind sounded like breakers crashing on that distant shore at Fort Clatsop, so far away.

THE END

Landmark

B O O K S